To Nia
Love you!
Shei, Calv
6-21-14

Why Should I Be Ashamed?

A memoir

By Sheila Perry-Calvert

Revised Edition

Foreword by De'Vonna Bentley-Pittman

ISBN-13: 9781499366563
ISBN-10: 1499366566

Dedicated to my amazing husband,

Anthony Allen Calvert

Foreword

As an author, editor, and a survivor of sexual abuse, I salute Sheila Perry-Calvert. She has been victorious, and her memoir is proof that abuse can't hold you back from God's blessings or His healing. She gives hope to those who are still struggling with the effects of physical and sexual abuse. For many years she carried secrets that were eating away at her core. In her very raw memoir—*Why Should I be Ashamed*, she shares pieces of her journey in an effort to allow others to heal and experience the freedom God has graciously granted her with. This triumphant story gives hope to individuals who have been abused and seemingly forgotten.

Why did God allow these horrible things to happen to her? Why was she born into a life of abuse and shame? How was she able rise above the abuse and to walk in freedom and forgiveness? She struggled to answer those questions growing up, but now boldly tackles them in her memoir *"Why should I be Ashamed"*.

Now, an empowered advocate, Sheila seeks to educate, counsel, and mentor those affected by sexual abuse - including those who watched in silence.

Sincerely,

De'Vonna Bentley-Pittman

"Author of My Pretty...and Its Ugly Truth"

Introduction

From My Heart to Yours

I endured much pain and many tears when I finally began to write about my childhood. I had many mixed emotions, and at first I was ashamed and apprehensive. Although I needed to share my truths, I wondered how people would perceive me. Perception is everything, right? In the past when I'd shared the details of my life, some people were critical and suggested that I should have just "run away," or they simply expressed what they would have done had they been in my situation.

I've learned that we all have different experiences and ideals, but no one can truly say what they would have done, unless they were in my situation. As a young girl I was frightened and confused with no answers to any of my questions and no real help or support. I shared my story with the world to express how abuse can affect the mind, and the future of a child.

Our society hasn't spoken to the issues of child abuse at the level of its destruction, and it is absolutely one of the world's overlooked problems. I'm led to believe that most people think that if they turn a blind eye on the crimes against children, somehow they will go away. If they pretend it never happened, the child will grow up and forget about it. That is so far from the truth. Children never forget! I never forgot! One thing I'm sure of is this, if bystanders don't address sexual abuse it will eventually manifest into something dreadful. I am a witness that if sexual abuse isn't addressed it has the potential to erupt like a cancer, lying dormant for many years and then all of a sudden it has affected many areas of one's life.

We need to do something to bring security to every child everywhere. Our streets are filled with people who were victims of child abuse. Our criminal justice system consistently fills up prisons with people, who have at some point in their childhood been victims of sexual abuse. Statistics show that 60% of prisoners have had at least one or more sexual abuse experiences. Sexual abuse is like a secret society that no one wants to talk about or be affiliated with, so many people hide it. Most are too embarrassed to admit it happened to them.

Writing one's truth forces the writer to live that truth all over again. It is with a sincere passion for those who are hurting, that I reveal my own truths. This journey was birthed from my desire to see a generation set free from the shame of abuse. Initially, I wanted to "testify". I wanted to tell the world how I lived through the tragic, raging storms of life, and how I overcame them. As I began to write, I felt it was rather important and relevant to uncover the shame that I had become protective of. Yes, I had subconsciously allowed myself to harbor shame, as if I had brought the abuse upon myself. After many years, I finally asked, 'Why should I take the blame? Why should I be ashamed?'

The Lord has given me the strength to overcome my shame, but I experienced the hurt, embarrassment, and bitterness that that abuse brings. I still find myself uncovering layers of hidden residue, including abandonment and neglect as a result of having been abused. Through all of that, I have come to realize that there is healing for everyone who wants it and believes they can walk in complete healing and freedom.

I realized many years ago that I'm not alone. I declare that all over the world, the day will come when children will seek help and they will be able to find it. I have declared that I will not be smothered by internal shame, and by sharing intimate details of my life; I'm declaring that others will be free also.

I've been transparent in my writing, by revealing my own struggle and my desire to survive.

Sincerely,

Sheila Perry-Calvert

Chapter 1

In the Beginning

I can still envision my Uncle Woody's house. I've had a picture of that house in my mind for many years. I will never forget the big reddish-brown brick building on the corner of Burlingame Avenue. The house was centered in a very classy neighborhood on the west side of Detroit, Michigan. I'll never forget the address where I was born – 3046 Burlingame. The lawns were fabulous and welcoming- - thick, and as green as new money.

Uncle Woody was successful in my eyes; he lived in a nice home and drove nice luxurious cars. As a child, I believed he was a man of wealth, but I eventually realized he was a hard worker who managed his finances well, and it paid off for him. Uncle Woody was my role model and I looked up to him. I loved Uncle Woody, and it was *his house* that will always have a place in my heart and memory. Uncle Woody's house was the origin of where it all began. My soul is rooted deeply within the walls of that house.

After stepping foot inside 3046 Burlingame as an adult, I could still smell the strong aromas of greens, fried chicken, roast beef, and piping hot cornbread. When I visited my uncle's house, I remembered things from my childhood. The scents lingered in my memory and took me back through a time warp of sorts. This is the house where it all began. Looking back through the tunnel of life, I can still see Uncle Woody leaning back in his brown La-Z-Boy chair, smoking his pipe and wearing his plaid robe with that proud, accomplished look on his face. He didn't have a care in the world, and I knew it because he never complained about anything. His wife, Aunt Lily was a quiet woman. That was the side of my family I loved and was proud to be a part of, until Mama began to tell me family secrets. She said that while on his deathbed, my grandfather begged my aunts not to let his two orphan children fall into the hands of his brother, Uncle Woody. My grandfather, Joseph Perry Sr. knew something about his brother that no one else knew.

I loved my mother. We were so much alike – both shy and wary of confrontations. She was a beautiful woman. My mother was thin, with jet-black hair, her skin was soft and she had a deep brown complexion. Mama had big brown eyes and thinner lips. She shaved her eyebrows perfectly and then she'd pencil in any sparse spots. When she was finished, her eyebrows were perfect and she looked just like the movie stars I had seen on television back when television was black-and-white.

Even before my siblings and I were born, we were destined to have a chaotic journey through life. It happened because of the broken foundation that had been laid long before we were thought of. It's true, most children do what they're taught, but there are a few of us who abhor our upbringing so much that we pray, even as children, things will be different for our own unborn children. It is then, by divine intervention that we escape our childhood tragedies. It was obvious that Mama didn't escape her tragic childhood.

Mama moved from Detroit to Alabama, shortly after she met and married a man named Charlie. She really liked him and he seemed to be a family man. Charlie had sisters and brothers who made Mama feel as if she would finally inherit a sense of family. They accepted Mama, and me as well. When Mama gave birth to the twins; Marquetta and Kirk, they loved them too. The acceptance from Charlie's family couldn't resolve the issues that they had created by diving into a marriage immaturely. The marriage was strained from the very beginning. Mama explained to me that she had only gotten married to leave Uncle Woody's house because she felt unloved and unprotected there.

Unfortunately, the marriage wasn't much of an escape for Mama. During her time with Charlie, my ten-month-old baby sister Marquetta, died. We had heard that "a grain of rice had lodged into her intestine and caused her to become very ill and dehydrated". My parents took her to the doctor, but back then things were different. According to the accounts of family members, southern white physicians had no empathy for black patients. All it would have taken to make my sister better was a simple IV, but the white southern doctor demanded my parents pay up or plain and simple -- he could not help them. Mama said that by the time they went up the hill to get the money and made it back to the hospital her precious baby girl Marquetta was gone. The tragedy was another wound in Mama's spirit, a wound for which she never fully recovered from.

We eventually moved away from the South and journeyed to Chicago to live with Charlie's sister, Aunt Mae. Aunt Mae was married with eight children of her own. She was a nurse, a homemaker, and the sweetest soul you could ever meet. After we moved into Aunt Mae's house, there were always conflict between Mama and Charlie, and we witnessed many heated exchanges of words.

Aunt Mae mediated between the young couple quite often, but Charlie and Mama were destined for failure. They eventually separated, and we were soon on our own in the big city of Chicago. Somewhere in her losses, Mama personalized her sad experiences and eventually devalued her self-worth and settled for whatever physical, mental, or emotional hardship that came her way. She didn't seem to care or have any fight left in her. She carried on as if she was immune to pain, but there were times I'd over hear her ask God why had there been so much hardship in her life. My mother began to drink to cope with life and to cover the disappointments. She drank to forget the past, and to deal with her bleak future.

I am by no means making excuses for my mother's choices. In sharing my mother background you may see clearly where the root of my pain comes from. Like so many people with wounded spirits, her troubled past and hard experiences, caused her to live a life of depression with many unresolved issues. Somewhere in her loss, her self-worth was destroyed. Mama felt so devalued that she settled for whatever attention came her way. Her broken spirit overflowed into every relationship she encountered. Her low self-esteem damaged her marriage, her ability to be a good mother and every aspect of life. Her expectation was limited, and she always anticipated the worst. I don't recall her having faith in anyone or anything.

Watching through the eyes of a child, I promised myself I would never let my disappointments change who I was really meant to be.

Chapter 2

Total Surrender

It had been my first day of elementary school, and walking home seemed to take much longer that day for some reason. The sun was shining and I was excited about how the day had gone, it had been bright and lively. Everyone had said that I looked so pretty in my pink dress and pigtails. Mama walked me to school that morning so my first day was bound to be extraordinary. I felt loved. My teacher had laid out a long piece of white paper on the floor to trace the shape of my body. I felt special as I stretched out my three-foot-long body on top of it while she drew a silhouette of my small frame. As the day went on, I was in a world of my own with my creative imagination as I colored, played, and learned. I imagined childhood being great every day after that.

Mama picked me up from school that day around 3:15 p.m. I immediately noticed the bottle of Coke in her hand. Mama loved her coke; it was her midday drink following her morning cup of Folgers coffee. As we walked home, a tall, brown-skinned man whistled at Mama. She began to blush and smile as if she was the catch of the day. Mama was a very classy lady and had a sense of charm, and I'm sure he was drawn to her beauty. Her black hair was as shiny and fine as a rich lady's mink coat. She pressed and curled it, and the curls seemed everlasting; you couldn't even brush them out. The tall man looked at her and smiled, and then asked my mother for one sip of her Coke. She held it up the coke bottle, as if to say, 'Sure you can have it all, I surrender all'. He was a six-foot, brown-skinned, good-looking man with pretty teeth, and dressed nicely for a poor man assumingly living in our poor neighborhood back in the 60's.

We didn't realize that one whistle and a wink of the eye would change our lives forever. That moment put a new spin on the familiar warning about not talking to strangers. My mother quickly became very acquainted with the man we all came to know as "Los," and they eventually became an item. He spent many nights at our apartment. Then out of nowhere Mama alerted me that we were moving and I would be going to a new school on the west side of Chicago. My mom's new boyfriend became friendly with us children, and we believed he was a nice person. He showed me favoritism over all the other children.

Meet the family

They were all scary-looking, or maybe I was just nervous meeting them for the first time. That's how I remember the scene when we walked into Los' family's home. I remember standing very still and very close to Mama as if I didn't want to part from her. Los had brought Mama and me to meet his family. Mama was "sharp as tack," and so was I. I wore a dress with the exact same pattern as Mama's. I can still visualize my mother in that moment, she was thin and beautiful with jet black hair and a W-cut neckline, she wore pointed toed high heels and a white dress with green flowers. The dress stopped at her knee, with a pleated inverted split down the back. My dress was adorned with the same pattern, but I wore black patent leather shoes with fluffy white socks. My hair hung past my shoulders in Shirley temple curls all over my head.

Everyone stood around staring as if we were specimens. It appeared as if everyone had been playing outside all day, even the adults, they were all sweaty and dusty-looking. I felt so out of place. This was clearly another world, a very different world that we hadn't been accustomed to. I had never seen anything like this.

The children loved me; they seemed so happy to see a beautiful woman and a child. They played with me as if I were some precious ruby or a doll sent from above to play with them. They even fought over me. Most of Los' family members had very dark complexions, which made me stand out even more. From that day forward, I was called "yellow," meaning I had very light-skin. Back in those days the very separation of complexion stirred up secret rivalries, secret hate, and forbidden secret love. If you were lighter complexion you were either shown favoritism or people secretly hated you. I was hated by most of the adults from the very beginning. Regardless of my complexion, I would later be inducted into the family's world of secrets and perversion.

Netta, who was the daughter of Los's sister, eventually became my first best friend. She was beautiful, with gorgeous, naturally curly hair that she put water and oil on to make it shine. Everyone wanted silky hair like Netta's. She had big, bright Diana Ross eyes, nice teeth, and she knew how to have fun. She was the youngest of her siblings, and the most humble and kindest of them all. Netta was taller than I was and she was very strong – not because she was a tomboy either, she was just strong from being around all the men in her family. I loved hanging with Netta, she made up games for us to play and was always finding fun things for us to do. She had lots of friends in the neighborhood, so we played hopscotch and jumped Double Dutch for hours. We were just like other children in the neighborhood and we liked to have fun. We loved eating gigantic pickles while using peppermint sticks as our straw to sip the pickle juice. Everyone loved Netta – both the girls and the boys. One time, her mother Nadine let her spend the night with me, and we stayed up all night giggling and whispering. We caught bugs kept them in a jar, and when the lights went out we took a candle and set fire to them. We never got caught.

Netta and I got along just fine – that is, until the jealous teenagers coerced us into fighting like two pit bulls. They commanded us to fight and we were too young to know any better. We did as we were told and scratched up each other's faces as we fought like cats and dogs. I wasn't sure if this was a game Netta had played with them before, but I didn't like it. Fist fighting was never in my heart and I never understood what kind of evil people would make best friends fight. Things got worse when Nana "took my side" after she heard how I had to fight two sisters. She said, "Sheila would whip their tails!" This caused Nadine to become furious because it had become obvious that she did not like me, so she was determined to provoke fights. She cussed and made a scene until everyone was ready to fight. Nadine was full of gangster rage, so it didn't take much to get her started, as always she got upset at any hint of opposition. Nadine hated my mother and I because Nana enjoyed spending time with us. I was sure that there was no affection shown during Los and Nadine's childhood and that Nana may have rejected them emotionally when they were children. Nadine never showed her mother any respect and in eighteen years I never saw them exchange hugs or kisses, and there were never any kind words. It was as if they'd created their own love language, and it consisted of pulling out guns, cussing each other out, and being disrespectful. Strangely, Nadine and Nana wouldn't allow anyone else to do this to their family members without a fight.

It was odd to me that after Mama and Los had been dating for a while we continued to refer to him as Los, but he referred to us as "his children". I remember trying to call him daddy, but it never felt right, something was missing. He wasn't my father and he wasn't a father figure. Los had children of his own and my mother embraced them. She welcomed them into our home, and one of his sons even lived with us at one time. We loved his children as if they were our own blood. His youngest daughter and I looked and acted as if we were from the same mom and dad, we truly loved each other. We never took our anger for him out on each other.

Chapter 3

A New World

As children, we didn't understand how evil Los really was, we looked up to him at first, and early on we accepted his toughness as representation of a protector. Mama wanted to see the good in Los, and it was obvious that she believed that good lived in him somewhere. She also wanted someone to repair the pain in her heart, the pain of her past. I'm sure she didn't know what to look for in a man because sadly she'd never had a good representation to mirror what a good man was. I don't know if she really considered what kind of father he would make, or if he was even ready for the responsibility that came along with being her man. For a while, we were impressed with

Los because he seemed to be a protector. Mama mistook his dominating behavior as a lion protecting his cub, but it was far from that, Los was a very dark and angry man.

We moved into a three-story flat with Los that had a long hallway and a dark stairway that led to the second floor. There was a living room when you first entered the apartment, and directly to the left were a bedroom, a bathroom, and another bedroom with French doors; Mama reserved the room with the French doors for my little brother Kirk. My sister and I shared a bedroom in the rear of the apartment near the back door by the sun porch and the back yard which had no grass.

We initially had some fun times and Los seemed to genuinely accept and care about us all. Back then, we believed we finally had a normal family. We made a makeshift baseball field by transforming the backyard.

I was in the third grade on my way to the fourth; that is, if I could survive the fights my sister had gotten into. Rhaquel was only in kindergarten, but she was a spitfire! Since I was the oldest, it was my responsibility to make sure my little brother and sister got home safely every day. Rhaquel was a thin girl with short hair, and for some reason the other kids just didn't like her. She didn't like them much, either. Rhaquel was feuding with someone more days than she wasn't.

Pee-wee was a neighborhood bully who had become our biggest enemy. I was a prissy little girl who would never in a million years initiate a fight or even imagine balling up my fists to hit someone. I didn't even want to imagine having scratches on my face. Not to mention, I was very timid, like my mother. I imagine being timid was a safe place for her. She didn't like controversy, and I don't ever remember her fighting or arguing with anyone. I never blamed Mama; she hadn't ever had any one to stand up for her.

I'm reminded of the day my brother, sister, and I were walking home from school. It was very hot and muggy that afternoon. Our favorite past time when no adults were around was "cussing," all the way home from school, we would cuss until we entered our doorway unless mama or Los were standing on the porch. Of course we knew better, but it gave us an outlet and allowed us to express ourselves in a bold and aggressive way without getting in trouble. We had become fearful of Los, and had begun to bottle up the anger deep inside our hearts. Having the power to use vulgar language made us feel free. I think we all wanted to cuss Los right out of our lives, and we did, in our very own private cussing sessions. As we walked inside, I was shocked at what I saw; my mother's eye was badly bruised and swollen. I asked Mama what happened to her eye, and while I was caught up in my thoughts, Mama responded quietly that she had run into the doorknob. That was the first time I had ever seen Mama's face look like that, and I was horrified. My heart sank into my lap, and I didn't know what to say or do. The pure innocence of youth allowed me to justify and accept what Mama had just told me as the truth. It really did sound convincing, and like everything else

Mama had said to us we believed her when she fibbed about the black eye.

Even though we elected to believe our mother, there was still something very odd about that day, and on that day we all learned to be silent. The rest of the day was very quiet. We were all embarrassed and ashamed of the kind of life we were living behind closed doors. We didn't talk about it either, we were taught to stay out of grown folks business, so we figured they knew what they were doing, and they would figure it out. Even though, Mama sustained her injuries on the "door knob," she still stayed in the house so others wouldn't see it, and we continued going to school as if nothing happened. Even though Mama was home every day, she wasn't very active in the PTA and didn't attend school events. I still looked for her throughout the auditorium during our school programs, but she never showed up. Mama spent most of her time at home watching soap operas and sipping on coffee or Coke. She was still spending a lot of time with Los, despite the black eye he'd given her, and he was always around.

In those days, people referred to us a "ready-made family" because Mama had come into the relationship with children. We were far from a "happy family". Los seemed to be a nice person by day, but at night he was a tyrant. He was fierce and angry. We had begun to hear whispers about his drug addiction, and we knew that the drugs and alcohol only added fuel to the fire. Los seemed to have a desire to want to be a gangster or a pimp. He was the kind of man who took advantage of weak women and preyed upon little innocent girls and young boys whom he robbed of their manhood. He dominated our entire environment. When he walked through the apartment, the floors creaked, the walls crackled, and everything stopped crawling. He tried to portray himself as being fearless, but underneath it all he was a coward and he knew it. I thought everyone feared Los, I surely did. Just like Mama, we were all controlled by his madness. As a child, I'd wonder what he was so mad about. I wondered what could cause an individual to be mad every day, all year long; even during the summer months when the bright sun should have made us all smile.

Mama could no longer lie about the door knob because Los had begun to beat her on a regular basis and she regularly walked around with two black eyes and a swollen lip. Most times we were home, and witnessed the beatings and blood splattered throughout the house. We would scream, cry, and beg while kneeled in front of him, "Please, Los! Leave her alone!" We believed that if he didn't stop, he would kill her. After long nights of fighting, Mama was no match for him and she always lost. She was always the one who ended up beaten and battered. I believe that watching those scenes play out over and over again contributed to the stripping away of my brother's manhood and his self-worth. I think the beatings were harder on him because as a little boy, he wanted to be a man and defend his mother, but he was no match against Los' stature. He was defeated from the very beginning, and in the end it affected his mentality, his emotional stability and, ultimately his self-esteem.

I remember going to the doctor with Mama after one of her beatings and listening to her tell the doctor that a gang of boys had beaten her up. The doctor's reply was, "No gang members did this to you Mrs. Morgan." Mama dropped her head in shame. It was a very familiar scene for the doctor. He had heard other women accuse everyone, but their boyfriends. The doctor had seen so much of this kind of physical abuse in our neighborhood that it was a common experience for him. He gave Mama something for the physical pain, and she walked out of his office with her head held low, as she retreated back to the place where she had learned to accept defeat, and to deny the pain.

Aside from the beatings, there were several inappropriate moments with Los that stand out in my mind. Thinking back, I now know he was preparing my sister and I for what was to come when he took us to see "The Mack," a movie that focused heavily on prostitution, pimping, and street life. On another occasion, Los took Rhaquel to a hotel where he and some friends his age and older were shooting dice and drinking. Apparently, Los had tried to get the men there to pay him to have sex with my sister. Thank God the men were adamant that they would not have sex with a child. At that time Rhaquel was only 13 years old.

Statistics show that abusers will seek out women who are single with children. When Los met Mama, he must have thought he struck gold. He knew she didn't have any close relationships with family members and he made sure she didn't make any friends either. His violent moments of rage and his rudeness ensured that people would not befriend us.

In our case, many people turned their heads fearing the disapproval of the abuser. Many of us have seen this in our own lives. Bystanders sometimes believe that if someone is hurting you, you should take the initiative and find the strength to get out or to report the abuser to the authorities.

My mother found a man in the streets and she didn't have the full knowledge of his past, all she knew was that he had done a short stint in prison. With that limited knowledge, he brought him into our life and into our childhood without knowing who he was or what he was capable of doing. Mama never questioned his past and didn't know if he had been guilty of committing heinous crimes, or if he'd commit even worse crimes against her children. The unfortunate truth was that Los was a hurting individual who was practicing in a role he wasn't prepared for. The truth is that Los had spent much of his youth in the prison system, where he tried to be rehabilitated from past criminal behavior. Even during our childhood, he was always in trouble with either the law or one of the enemies he had made. It was obvious that he'd never had a role model or a father to teach him how to be a man, but now here he was, ill prepared to take care of another man's children.

Los had no respect for God and never mentioned Him either. I remember asking him a question about God once and his response was, "God is dog spelled backwards". From that point on, I believed a monster lived inside of him. One minute he would say unimaginable things to us, and the next minute he pretended to be loving and kind. There were even times when he declared, "I'm your father!"

There were always chaotic calamities following my "stepfather," such as the time he got shot in the leg and couldn't go to a doctor because he was a fugitive. Rather than get medical treatment he preferred to suffer in pain.

There were times when Mama had gotten the courage to leave Los, but it never lasted. One time she had gotten the locks changed to our apartment, but by the time we woke up that morning, we found Los fixing the lock on the door. Had Mama forgotten that he was the one she was locking out? Once again, she had given in to his deceptive devices and his apologies. Los had the ability to charm Mama and convince her that she was missing something and she would be alone and have to think for herself. Mama's desperate and lonely heart always gave in, and every time she allowed Los to convince her that he'd never hit her again, she welcomed fear back into our home. She didn't realize that each time she gave in to him; our lives became even more threatened. We never knew what to expect, what we did know was that Los had always promised to never hit Mama again.

It was rare that Los had civilized conversations with us. He explained to me (as if it hadn't been his own fault) that his youth and freedom had been terminated because of his juvenile delinquency, burglarizing, and staying in trouble. I believe that he felt justified in stealing our youth because he had missed out on his own. I was traumatized beyond belief when he looked me in the eye and said, "I didn't get to have young girls because I was in prison," I couldn't believe he had said those words to me and in some sick sort of way, he expected my pity!

When I think back to some of the things Los said and did I still find it hard to believe. He once told me that my mother had a "white liver, *nymphomaniac*" I wasn't sure what he meant.

Apparently, Mama had gotten her period and he was uptight and in need of sex. Although my mother knew his comments were highly inappropriate and made me very uncomfortable, she sat quiet and ignored them for fear of a beating. I usually ignored him and silently disappeared to another room. Los made me sick to the stomach many days. Although I couldn't challenge his behavior, I never understood why a grown man would have such disgusting conversations with his fifteen year old step daughter. I knew this wasn't a normal, respectful conversation, but I couldn't do anything about it. More than anything, I wanted desperately to be a kid, but he was forcing me to think about sex. We dealt with these kinds of situations on a regular basis.

I really wanted to believe that Mama and Los were doing their best, but each day things seemed to be getting worse. Dreams were shattered day after day, and things never changed or got better. Sadly, our hopes were blinded by adults who were not exemplifying a future worth living for. Every day was an adventure of the worst kind. My favorite saying as a child was, "I can't wait until I'm eighteen so I can get away." I knew if I could just survive that life until they no longer had control over my choices I'd be okay. Everything I worked for and the choices I made would be far greater than what I'd seen. This gave me hope and reminded me that I could have a bright future. My belief that there was a God and He would get me through, kept me sane. I believed that God had a great big world out there for me and one day I'd get to experience it without fear and dysfunction. Those reminders kept me from taking my life on the days when I just didn't want to live any more.

Chapter 4
In This World Not of this World

If Nana moved to the West Side, Nadine and Los moved to

the West Side. If Nana moved to the suburbs, then the entire

family would eventually gravitate to that side of town. It had

become either a family tradition or a habit, but Los's family

always moved on the same side of town as their mother. Nana

was the matriarch of the family, and she was their rock. She

worked a twelve-hour a day job. Nana not only protected them,

she also protected all of their dirty little secrets. This made

them feel like they could get away with things, so they

continued with their unhealthy behaviors. Nana spent a lot of

time running to prison and county jail to bail her menaces out.

Cruelty was an understatement in this family; no one seemed to have a nice bone in their body. The men of that family did the same old rotten things to most of the people who came into their lives – especially women with insecurities and low self-esteem. I remember coming home from school one day to hear screams coming from the basement. It turned out to be a friend of Netta's, whose only weakness was marijuana and her desire to smoke a joint. She paid for that folly dearly -- all of her so-called friends stood around pacing the floor, while five men took turns raping her. I never understood why no one called the police, and I couldn't understand why the girl continued to befriend this family. My siblings and I had no choice; we were stuck with this family with no where to turn.

Most of the men in that family were always angry for no apparent reason. I witnessed them fight each other often and they usually didn't stop until someone bled. I even saw them pistol-whip a family friend, I'm still not sure what he did but they beat him right in our kitchen. Some of them would steal from anyone who laid anything down. Young adults and teens in Los' family perpetrated much of the violent behavior. They thought the whole world owed them something for all of their unresolved issues. They fought and took it out on anyone who was in their space. I once saw them walk up to an innocent bystander and physically attack the person, while Nana yelled using expletives "Beat their - - - !" I remember picking up a pile of 45 records and furiously throwing them all over their house after being shoved into a rage by one of the family members. As if their violent behaviors weren't enough for bloody entertainment, they usually waited until the adults went out at night so they could make the younger kids fight. They loved to see someone beating on me. They pushed Netta and me together until we punched each other to the ground and then they coerced their bigger sister Ressa to fight me as well. She was tall, with long arms and big feet, and I had to fight her. She wasn't much of a fighter, but she tried her best, she just couldn't fight. Fighting was not in her heart like it was in theirs, so they called us both cowards. They even humiliated us threatening to make us wear signs on our backs that said "COWARD". One time Nadine was so upset because I won the fight, that she got her gun out and tried to forced us to fight again. It was simple and there was no explaining it, our lives were chaotic most of the time.

Even in rare times of peace, we knew there was always a storm brewing. I have memories of me playing with the children in Los's family while the adults drank and listened to Motown 45's. The children all danced in a circle while singing "Chain of Fools." These moments were proof that we had a few good times sprinkled here and there. Friday night parties had become the family ritual. Sometimes the adults partied all night long until dawn or until someone started a fight. They drank until all of the adults were intoxicated from drinking the "ignorant water," as they often referred to liquor. Then, Nana would fuss and cuss and make a scene. I wasn't surprised when every now and then an adult got angry, turned around and pulled down their pants to tell one of the other partiers to "kiss where the sun didn't shine." Those kinds of episodes never surprised me; there was no telling what would happen when Los's family got together. I remember one Friday, Nana got so upset with Los that she said to my mother, "Grace, he's just waiting on Sheila to grow up!" She kept repeating it over and over. Los became infuriated at his mother for letting the cat out of the bag, and he gathered us all up and we left. A few years later, I found out that Los had been reporting my maturing sexuality and the development of my body to his mother. I was embarrassed to hear them fussing about my private growth.

Mama was really all we had and she had allowed Los to come in and take over our life and everything we owned. I had only met my father once while in Detroit, but it wasn't memorable. As bad as things were, Los was the closest thing to a father we had. He was a hustler and a gambler, and he had taken his time showing us who he really was. In the beginning he didn't cuss in front of us, and he didn't allow any other adults to use bad language in our presence. He seemed to be a decent person in the beginning and was likable when he wasn't drinking, but that was before we really knew him.

After Los moved in with us, he spent the day walking back and forth through the house as if he were the warden of a small jail cell. On Saturday mornings he didn't let us sleep in. He got up early in the morning and yelled for us to get up and clean the apartment. While Los was busy walking around the apartment, he made frequent trips into our bedroom. He was always sneaking around and hiding in the closet, transforming himself like a chameleon underneath the dirty clothing – pretending to be a concerned father trying to catch us misbehaving. One day, he came into our room, and we saw him. He then pretended to leave and slammed the door shut. I turned to my sister and said, "I hate him!" When I lifted up my head out of the bed, Los was standing there; he had only pretended to leave the room. I was so scared and unsure what would happen to me after those words loosely flew right out of my angry lips. I was afraid because by this time, I knew that Los was not to be disrespected by any of us. He rolled his eyes at me and walked out of the room.

Los was inappropriate most of the time and he spent the day commanding and controlling us. His favorite thing to do was to sit on the couch enforcing fear into all of our hearts. When we tried to watch television, he said things like, "I got to teach you all how to kiss." I was repulsed at the thought, 'who teaches their daughters such a thing?' Los told me over and over again that I was going to be a "bull dagger," because I wasn't having sex with him (or anyone else). He would repeatedly say, "I am the chief, you dig?" That was the power quote often used when he wanted to threaten us or our mother. When we became teenagers, he changed his quote to "If I go back to jail, it will be for murder or statutory rape." I had no idea what statutory rape meant, so I immediately went to the dictionary to look up his new choice word. When I found out that statutory rape meant sex with a minor I was petrified. 'Who could that minor be?' I thought that the definition guaranteed that I was going to be raped. 'Had he been planning that from day one?' I was shocked that my mother would allow him to say such things in her presence. She sat there as if he hadn't said a word. The atmosphere he created was not fit for any normal person, and was surely unfit for a child.

Los was just as inappropriate with our friends as he was with us; he made lewd attempts at them, groped their behinds and even touched their breasts. He was out of control and it was obvious that he felt invincible. None of my friends every reported to their parents what Los did. I'm sure they were just as afraid of him as we were. We were all dealing with some form of dysfunction in our respective homes. Sexual abuse and incest was very prevalent, and I'm sure they were "grateful" to get away from Los without actually having been raped.

Chapter 5

An Undefined Love

Christmas was upon us and it was supposed to be a very special time for all of us. Even though we were practically living in poverty, we had great expectations. My brother got a nice train set that he loved, but unfortunately Los loved it too. He put it high up on a shelf so my brother couldn't get to it and would only take it down when he wanted to play with the "choo-choo" train. I'd gotten lots of candy, and a little brown-haired baby doll with blue eyes, and my sister got a blonde one. We spent the next few weeks coordinating tea parties with the dolls. Our imaginations had no limit -- I could be in a world outside of what I had known, especially at that moment – I could even be white like my baby doll, and no one would ever hit her. We were always looking for a way to escape our lives or to pretend as if nothing bad had ever happened to us or Mama.

Holidays were no exception for my mother's boyfriend's wrath. At Halloween, we went trick-or-treating for hours, but when we returned Los dumped out the bags of candy and took what he wanted. He allowed us to pick one piece each day for ourselves. We didn't have a say, so we allowed him to do the "fatherly thing" and regulate the amount of candy we ate. Even if in this instance, Los meant well, his previous actions wouldn't allow us to give him the benefit of a doubt. There had been too much abuse and negativity after he came into our life, and from where we stood, there was no good in him. We knew better than to say anything, because his response to any rebuttals was harsh and consisted of consisted of thumps or plucks in the head and vicious lies that he told my mom to justify his sick behavior. He grit his teeth to warn us that the monster was about to be released. Our childhood holidays were always bittersweet, full of drama, and very traumatizing for a child. We didn't know that the life we were living wasn't normal; we just knew it felt very painful, embarrassing and shameful.

Mama never had much to say, nor did she have a say in anything. I can remember one time when she tried to stand up for me. I had gone shopping for her at the neighborhood store, and as I was leaving, two teenage boys snatched the groceries and Mama's left over change right out of my hand! When I returned home and began to tell my mother what had happened, Los said, "She's lying. She was playing in the snow and lost the money." Mama jumped up and walked to the store on that cold wintery day. She asked the clerk if I had been there, and the clerk confirmed that I had been there and had in fact purchased the food. The clerk also told Mama that she'd seen two boys throwing snowballs outside the store. I was happy that Mama had heard the truth. It was as if she wanted to have some sort of say, even if it was in a vague sort of way. It was a small triumph, but it did no good. Los continued to repeat his chants over and over again "I'm the chief you dig," it was if we were in a brainwashing session. He had his own philosophy and his own language, and he was determined to convince us that he would have control, "Your mama can't think for herself," he often said. That was another one of his power quotes, "I have to think for her!" He said. One day I got up the nerve to remind him of how well mama thought for herself when we lived in Detroit without him. She was all we had, and I couldn't stand him belittling her all the time. One minute she was his common law wife, the next minute she was his punching bag. It didn't help that Mama had distanced herself from our family in Detroit and no longer had a relationship with them. I knew that underneath it all, Mama would have been embarrassed to be caught up with a man like Los.

Mama became a depressed alcoholic, she drank a lot and cried for long periods of time, and we often found her gazing into space while sitting in total silence. None of us children knew better than try to break her silence, so we watched helplessly as she became dependent on alcohol. The alcohol contributed to her mood swings. Sometimes after she had been drinking she became very nurturing and funny. During those times, she was very affectionate and gave us lots of hugs and kisses; it was as if she thought that she would get the same thing in return from Los.

Mama never lost the depth of character that we all believed lived deep inside her. We saw it on rare occasions when she still managed to show us love and in those moments when she tried to teach us to respect ourselves. Those moments assured us that we knew her spirit still lived in her body. Somewhere, within Mama, there was a voice and it made it easy to believe that one day Mama would overcome this and so would we.

Regardless of what we hoped would happen; Mama often struggled to exemplify the strength her father instilled in her. With everything she'd been through, there was still something amazing about my mother. Everything she touched came alive because she put her whole heart into it. Mama was a great housekeeper; she could cook, she could sew, and she was a good housekeeper. My mother was known for making girls beautiful with her knack for doing hair. She also loved to make people laugh, even at her own expense. She was gentle, and never called us derogatory names as I had seen so many parents do in the neighborhood I lived in. She was always affectionate, and charming. Mama had always taken extra care to make sure we were neat and clean. She believed that a woman's hair was her crown and glory, and ours was always perfect, so we always felt good about how we looked. I remember the nice warm baths Mama gave us, she even told us stories at night, after rubbing us down with Vick's Vapor Rub. I'm assuming the rub was supposed to help us sleep better.

Mama had a ritual of warming our pajamas by the oven, the warm pajamas and vapor rub, broke up the colds we had. Mama warm hands made us feel safe and secure. She tickled us until we got tired and dropped off to sleep. Mama made sure we washed our faces and brushed our teeth before we ate breakfast. Then we would all retreat to the kitchen for oatmeal and hot buttered toast. I didn't like the taste of oatmeal, so my brother always ate mine. This was our daily morning routine, Monday through Friday unless Mama was depressed or hung-over.

Everyone who met my mother liked her. She had an open heart, but when Mama was sober, she could be extremely grouchy and irritable, she needed her Budweiser.

Los didn't care that Mama felt alone or that she was depressed, in fact he used that very thing to make her feel even worse, "You think I'm going to feel sorry for you because you're crying and don't have a mother? I don't care about your situation." I remember Los taunting Mama as if it was yesterday. He gave no sympathy to her tears and there certainly was never an apology. Mama once told me that Los never apologized to her for anything he had ever done to her. Although she couldn't walk away or leave Los, Mama did regret it years later. I remember her saying to me, "I never should have let that man do what he did to my kids."

My mother didn't talk much about her childhood only that her grandma had sent them big baskets of fruit at one time or another. She said that she loved her daddy and her stepmother was very mean. Every now and then she reminisced on her memories of her stepmother. Mama talked a little about the time her stepmother forced her to sit out in the sun until she got sunburned. When her daddy finally made it home from work, he was livid at the way she had been treated by her stepmother -- my grandfather beat his wife to a pulp that day.

I had been introduced to an abusive childhood long before we met Los and long before my mother ever imagined her life spiraling out of control. The truth is, her unhealthy childhood played a role in her own life and created an atmosphere that she had become familiar with. My mother had allowed the same thing to happen to her that she had witnessed happening to her stepmother.

Chapter 6

New Year's Eve

Mama was still beautiful and when she wanted to get dolled up she could. She had a slim waistline to go with the tight-fitted skirt she wore. Her legs were shapely and looked great with her frame. She wore pointy toe high heel shoes and she looked great. She was on her way to the annual New Year's Eve party. Women wore shiny and sparkly hats that night, and we knew we would hear the horns honking and bullets shooting from celebratory guns. All of the adults looked forward to having big fun on that night as they looked to a New Year and a new future. It meant forgetting the past and hoping for something new.

While the adults partied and welcomed in a new year, Mama left us in the care of those immoral vultures, many of whom were half-grown perverts. They waited for us to fall asleep, only to wake us up in the middle of the night to take advantage of us. They were always watching and waiting for an opportunity to misuse us, and we were warned with a stern, "You better not tell."

Between the shame and the shock, we smothered our emotions and pretended as if nothing had happened to us. I never told my mother what really went on while she was out during the New Year's Eve celebration. That's another thing we had in common; keeping secrets. We subconsciously believed that those secrets would protect us, and like my mother, I was beautiful on the outside, but on the inside I was hiding a life of private pain and stories that have never been told, until now.

Mama was a stay at home mother and didn't work besides taking care of us, not in a traditional way, because Los didn't work either. I can't recall him ever being able to hold down a job. Once, he made an attempt at construction work, but quit after half a day. It was like the saying, "A jealous man can't work; neither can a raging man." He and Mama spent most of their time watching television, or tucked away in their bedroom. That is, until the first of the month – when Mama's welfare check arrived. Los was always anxious around that time of the month and hunted the mailman down. It was as if a paycheck was coming to pay him for being locked up in the bedroom all month long.

Things had gotten progressively worse and Los now even controlled Mama's food stamps and cash benefits. Mama submissively handed over her county benefits to Los every month, on one condition; she had to have her Budweiser. Every month, Los's mother demanded, that he let Mama control her own money, in hopes that he'd listen to her and hand over my mother's welfare check, but that never happened. As we'd been told over and over again, a man will only do what a woman allows him to do, and in this case, Los wasn't stopping any time soon.

The first of the month started out pretty much the same every month, Mama's check came, her and Los jumped in a cab to head to the grocery store. First, Los asked each of us what we wanted from the grocery store, as if he was going to make the "purchase" out of his own stash, and whatever we got we should be grateful for. He made it clear that it was a monthly treat, and we had better be thankful for what he was doing for us. He was also trying to distract us and make us forget about the ugly things we had experienced all month long.

The first of month was also a time for celebrating, and when Los and Mama had a few dollars, it was their turn to buy the Friday night drinks. We went to Nana's house to get the party started. While the adults were focused on their drinking and music, the older unattended teenagers were focused on their sexual plans for us younger kids and what they would do to us. Once the drinking started, the adults elevated into a world of their own. They wanted to separate the children from the adults while, "grown folks were talking," The language was either hyper-political or hyper- sexual, not a conversation for children, but as usual these conversations always escalated into hard feelings which manifested into anger that inevitably filled the air.

Los had taken control of Mama's welfare checks for several months, but somehow she had gotten the strength to walk away from it all. The controlling behavior had gone on for far too long, and one day when Los got drunk and fell asleep, Mama decided to get us out of there. She picked his pockets for her own money, and told us to hurry up and get dressed. I can't remember how we got downtown to the Greyhound bus station so fast, we were just glad that Mama was free of Los and we were finally free of him too. We were so happy to be on our way to Detroit! It was as if we could hear Martin Luther King

Jr. saying to us, "Free at last, thank God almighty, we are free at last!"

When we made it to Detroit, we had such a sense of peace, and I can't explain the sense of relief we encountered. We skipped and hopped for the first time in ages. Oh, what joy! As we were walking I remember seeing a pair of black patent leather shoes in a display window in town. I wanted them so badly, and Mama bought them for me, brand new, right out of the display window. It had been a long time since I'd gotten something new.

I don't recall the reaction of our family in Detroit or if Mama even consulted with them. We stayed at the shelter for women and children for a couple of days, and then they made us go to the Grand River Hotel. The next thing I knew, I was awakened out of what seemed like a dream. We were on our way back to Chicago. Los had found Mama again, and to our dismay she had given in to his tactics, Mama had fallen for the false promises again. Mama had to have been talking to Los on the phone for this to happen. Maybe she'd never stopped talking to him at all, and in our oblivion and excitement we didn't know the difference. We were all so excited about being away from Los that we never imagined Mama would take him back. We were not happy, but there was nothing we could do.

It didn't take long for Los to return back to his abusive ways, in fact, it was immediate. We went to school the next day, and when we returned home, we found Mama beaten once again. She looked like Donald Duck's profile, her lips were swollen and she had two black eyes, Mama had lumps all over her head and her head shook nonstop. My stomach ached to see Mama like that. I hated that man, and I hated everyone who knew about my mother's situation and did nothing to help. Mama had been beaten so badly that she suffered enormous trauma from the beating. She had a nervous breakdown and was admitted to the hospital. If there was a tiny morsel of affection for Los, after that day it was completely gone. He had no compassion for our mother. I'd seen my mother beaten as if she were not even human.

Nana and the family stood and watched our situation play out every day without saying a word. Nana couldn't change who her children had become even if she tried. I had questions that no one could answer and I dared not ask them aloud. 'Why had Mama returned to Chicago? Why did Los hate Mama so much? Why didn't anyone stop him?'

After Mama returned from the hospital the beatings didn't stop. A few weeks Later, Los was upset about something and went into the kitchen and grabbed a knife. Mama came screaming into my bedroom and snatched me up out of my sleep and held me in front of her as a shield. I was petrified and frozen in disbelief – 'She'd rather him kill me than her?' For what seemed like an eternity, I was her armor. Mama stood there crying as she held me in front of her, "Put her down and let her go to bed," Los said. Finally, Mama put me down and I was allowed to go back to bed. The next morning I got up and went to school, where I was expected to get all A's. When I made it home from school, I was shocked to find that Mama was angry with me. She even had the audacity to say that my sister Rhaquel would have never left her alone up there with the monster. I was confused. Mama had shifted the blame from Los to me! It was safer to be upset with me, but she better not dare show any anger toward Los. It was in that moment Mama had solidified a rivalry between my sister and I, and it guaranteed that the sisterly bond we shared would be severed. My mother had insinuated that Rhaquel was loyal and I wasn't. Mama turned us against each other, and though it had never been verbally expressed – this too was due to our very different skin tones. I blamed my little sister for my mother's hatred toward me in that moment. I allowed my mother to put division in my heart. It had always seemed that she favored Rhaquel anyway. I was the strong one, and maybe Mama didn't like me because she wished she had the strength I had.

Chapter 7

No Calm After the Storm

Los went to jail for two years when I was approximately ten or eleven years old. Mama later told us she had prayed to God for him to get locked up. Unfortunately, Mama had become so co-dependent on Los that when he went to jail, she couldn't cope and her drinking problem became even worse. She drank until she became even more deeply depressed than she already was. While Los was in jail his family ruled our house and they were there quite often, sometimes spending many nights at a time. Mama eventually lost total control of our apartment to Los's family, and they took over our apartment. They brought their boyfriends and girlfriends over to have sex, and they had parties and ate all of our food. As they raided our refrigerator and controlled our apartment, we had become severely neglected. Mama was usually nowhere to be found and, she wouldn't come home for days at a time. Our apartment became infested with rats, roaches, and teenagers. We never had food – not even the toast and oatmeal we'd been accustomed to. The pretty hairdos had become a thing of the past and we had to learn to take care of ourselves because Mama was never at home, it seemed. Los's relatives were supposedly looking after us until she returned in the evening. Some nights we ended up at Nana's house.

One cold blustery day we had awakened after spending the night at Los's sister's house, and were preparing to go to school once again without Mama's presence. Mama was probably still out from the night before, she had a tendency of staying out all night with her friends. As I prepared to go to school, I couldn't find my boots and it had become obvious that someone had moved them on purpose. I remember all the other children going to school that morning, and suddenly the house was silent. My brother and I continued to search for my boots to no avail; we were baffled, because we couldn't find them anywhere. I later discovered that two of Los's brothers "my uncles" and their friends were guilty and had plotted against me. That morning the sixteen and seventeen year old boys watched me like a tiger trapping its prey as I hunted for my boots. All of a sudden, those two so-called "uncles" and one of their friends appeared after all the other children had left for school. The boys held me down, and sexually assaulted me. I screamed as they forced themselves on top of me. My little brother was forced to watch helplessly. He was shocked and didn't know what to do. He had no idea they had schemed and planned this act against me. No one came to my rescue. I cried with shame and fear. My brother and I didn't go to school that day, we were both in shock.

When Nana came home from work that evening, I told her what had happened, but she cussed me out and yelled at the top of her lungs, "You stayed home from school because you wanted them boys to play in your pu--y. I should whip your black a--! You liked it. Now take your --- home!" I'm not sure what I expected Nana to do, maybe I thought for once she'd help me or she would stand up for what was right. I was so embarrassed and ashamed that I couldn't even breathe. I couldn't believe what had come out of that woman's mouth, and she had looked at me as if I were a piece of trash. I could tell she wanted to whip me with the same extension cord she used on her children. After Nana's reaction, I couldn't bring myself to tell my mother, I was too ashamed. This wasn't new though, Nana had always covered up her sons' dirt. They were horrible, always doing something and going to jail or in some other kind of trouble. Nana had created menaces to society, and she never reprimanded her sons to my knowledge for the vicious rape. All of her anger was directed towards me. Did anyone tell her that those monsters had hidden my boots? Did she even ask if I was hurt? No. She simply covered it up with a few curse words and pretended that her sons had done no

74

wrong. I was numb for the next few days. I didn't know how to sustain a blow like that. My brother and I have never discussed that day, and as usual we went on with life as if nothing had happened. I expected that one day I'd get an apology for the pain and abuse from my "uncles," but I never did, and I had to find solace deep within my soul. Something kept telling me that it would be okay and one day I'd find peace from my pain and suffering.

We had endured some pretty tough times up to this point, but the day we had all been waiting for had come, Mama finally sobered up. She took her welfare check and we were Detroit bound on the Greyhound once again. We didn't realize that Mama had gone to visit Los in prison and he had heard that she had lost complete control over our apartment and demanded she move to Detroit to be with her family. We were tired, confused, neglected, and abused. I can't imagine what mama was feeling. Her dangerous man was in prison, she had three children, no job, and once again, she had no one to turn to. We went to the same shelter as before, and eventually got an apartment. Life was okay. Mama had come to herself again and things were looking up. She took us to the doctor to get physicals and even though we had to get shots, we were happy. The hospital was bright, clean, and peaceful, we were in Detroit and that's all that mattered to us. No more darkness and no more fights.

We moved to Woodward Avenue, where we lived above a bar. Mama made a few friends who were single with children like her, and we became friends with their kids. Mama got a part-time job for a while, but when she wasn't around we displayed mischievous behavior that I'm sure was a direct result of all we'd been through. Either way, we'd begun to act out and mama didn't have anyone to care for us or make sure we behaved while she worked. She quit her job and became a stay-at-home mom once again.

One day mama took us shopping and bought us brand new clothes from Sears & Roebuck. I'll never forget our "angel dresses". My sister's was silky and pure white, and mine was a soft pale pink. They were brand new, right off the rack. It was a big deal to us because in Chicago, we wore second hand clothes that were usually too big or worn out. To finally have a chance to wear a brand new dress meant a lot to me. I felt like I belonged in beautiful things, I loved them, and it was obvious that the ghetto life had not stripped me of my desire for nice things or of my self-worth.

I knew I didn't belong there in the ghetto, in poverty – with the poverty thinking. The children in Chicago would often tell me I wasn't related to them and there was no way their blood ran through my veins. I didn't behave as they did, I was different. I knew I was someone special even in the midst of all the turmoil. I knew that there was a God who had made me special and given me a purpose in life.

Chapter 8

Abandoned Love

While we were in Detroit we met blood relatives we hadn't known before the move to Chicago. Auntie Virgie, Auntie Odyssey, and Cousin Simon Perry Sr. & Jr. were some of the family we met. Mama knew that it was important for us to know who and where we came from, and it made us feel proud to know that we came from good stock. Our aunts and cousins had nice homes with beautiful lawns. My mother's family was the polar opposite of Los's family; they were educated, hard-working, and kind people. I'm sure if they had known about the things we endured under the hand of Los and his family they wouldn't have been happy.

Things had been going well, but for some reason Mama decided to take a weekend visit with her friend Frances to Chicago. We didn't understand why she had to go, but we weren't worried about her being with Los because he was still in prison. My mother didn't want her family to know that she'd once again taken off and gone to Chicago, so she asked Mr. Rueben to take us. She left us in the care of her neighbor Mr. Rueben and told him that she would return the following Sunday. Although Mama trusted Mr. Reuben, there was something strange about him. I couldn't quite put my finger on it; maybe it was my own discomfort with men because of my history of abuse and not being able to trust men. Mama trusted Mr. Rueben because he played cards with her and her friends. They spent many long nights gambling for money. His girlfriend Michelle came over often to hang out a few times, and I was happy about that because I think it took his attention off my sister and I. We spent three days with Mr. Reuben, and I was thankful to God because I was sure that he would try to force himself on my sister and I. I was used to the men in my life taking advantage of us, so I didn't expect him to be any different.

That Sunday we all expected Mama to return and we were happy because we missed her, but Sunday came and went and mama didn't return. Mr. Rueben hadn't planned on us having to stay with him so long, so eventually he said, "You have to go home now…I can't take care of you all anymore. Your mama didn't call. I don't know what's going on, but you can't stay here." He gave us the key to our place and we went home.

I did the best I could to take care of my sister and brother, and I waited patiently for Mama to come home, because I believed she would. In my heart, I just knew she loved us, and I knew as soon as she sobered up, she'd come home. My mom's friend, Ms. Veronica, came over to comb our hair for school once or twice, but by the third day she couldn't take care of us any longer, besides she had her own children to care for.

I took my brother and sister home each day after school and locked the door, letting no one in and no one out. We looked out of the window and down at the bar until late in the wee hours of the night. The Detroit pimps and players stood in front of the bar showing off their clothes and their Afghan Hounds. For some reason these dogs had become popular to these thugs, but I liked watching the dogs because they were more graceful than their owners. Rhaquel and I teased and argued over the sharply dressed men, going back and forth about which one of them belonged to us. I'd pick out the most handsome one and say, "He's mine," and she'd snap back, "No, he's mine". This went on until the bar closed at 2:00 a.m. We usually stayed up really late hoping Mama would show up at some point. The pimps and players came and went, but still no Mama, so we eventually dozed off to bed. One afternoon, we were home on the couch, and a lady knocked on the door. I looked out the door and was suddenly afraid. I knew it was serious because white people didn't come to our house or our

neighborhood unless there was a perfectly good reason.
"What do you want?" I asked as I peeked through the keyhole.
"I want to talk to your mother," the lady responded. "She's not here, she went to the store". I said confidently.

I was so proud of myself for being quick on my feet. "Okay, I will come back tomorrow." she said hesitating. She looked around the front of our apartment and headed to her car. I assumed it was Veronica who called Child Protection Services and told them we were alone. 'If only we had a telephone,' I thought. I knew that if we had a phone in our house Mama would have called us by now.

The next afternoon, the white lady came to our apartment again. This time, she called me by my name. "Sheila, your mother is not at the store. I want to help you," she said. There was no food in the house and we were hungry. I'd had enough. It had already been three days and I didn't want to be in the house alone without an adult another night. I opened the door, and there she stood – a social worker. The social worker took us to an orphanage nearby where we saw children of different ethnicities. It turned out that I was the oldest in the group. We had dinner with the other children, took baths, and were shown to our rooms. The Social worker said we would be in foster care and hopefully end up living with a relative, a friend, or someone who would be willing to keep us together until they heard from our mother. Her first responsibility was to find suitable housing for us and to make sure we continued our education. The next morning we got up really early. I wasn't too fond of the oatmeal with raisins and it was evident, but I found out quickly that if you didn't eat your breakfast, you didn't get a treat. Every day we had the same breakfast, and every day, it was a reminder that Mama still hadn't come for us.

All of the children from the orphanage walked to school together daily and we were getting used to our new normal. While we walked down the street the neighborhood kids teased us spewing out insults, "Our mothers would never give us away!" they said. Those things hurt to the core, but we learned to ignore it. I knew Mama couldn't have possibly given us away because she loved us and we loved her. Yes, I was smart enough to know that she had neglected us, but give us away? No, Mama would never do that. In fact, she told me she wanted to leave us on someone's door step, but had decided she couldn't live without us. So, 'why would she leave us now?' I thought.

Although we were in the midst of strangers, we were grateful for the sense of security. We didn't know where we would end up or what the next steps to our foster care placement would be, but after a month or so, Mama still hadn't showed up. We continued to attend school and adjust to our new life, and in our minds we were doing just fine.

One day we returned to the orphanage from school and all of the girls' hair was cut off. When I asked why all the girls' hair had been cut off, Ms. Mary, the staff member nonchalantly said, "We don't know what to do with it. It will be more manageable this way". Most of the women who worked at the orphanage were white and they had no idea how to care for African American hair. Our hair required conditioning and daily maintenance; something my mother knew how to do very well. I begged Ms. Mary not to cut my hair off. The neighborhood children would surely make fun of my new short hair. Ms. Mary promised me that she wouldn't cut my hair as short as the other girls. Although, I'd never considered my hair a problem, her justification was firm, "It would be easier to manage if it was cut a little lower."

All the girls seemed to get over their haircuts eventually, and we realized that the orphanage wasn't bad at all. Actually, it was rather peaceful. The children got along pretty well and there was no domestic violence or sexual abuse occurring there. All of us were from different backgrounds, but had experienced similar dysfunction, so we related to one another. We each shared stories of why we had come to the orphanage, and were instantly bound together by our respective stories.

Since I was the oldest child there, I helped bathe the others and combed their hair. Sibling groups shared bedrooms so I was still helping to take care of my sister and brother. We were adjusting to our new normal; we were given new clothes, pajamas, slippers, and clean sheets. There were no spankings and we received three meals day. We even went on field trips occasionally to places like the county fair and the circus. Those things took our minds off our families for a short time, and the friends we made felt like an extended family.

One evening, when we were getting ready for bed Ms. Mary called my siblings and me downstairs. To our shock Mama and Uncle Woody were standing at the end of the stairs waiting to see us! We screamed and ran into Mama's arms. We were surprised and happy. We exhibited a range of emotions that evening when we laid eyes on our mother. We cried and laughed, we were so happy to see our long lost mother. Mama hugged and kissed us with tears falling from her face. She flooded our faces with tears and held us tighter than ever. It seemed Mama didn't want to let us go. She noticed that our hair had been cut and we could tell she didn't like it one bit. She seemed really happy to see us.

After Mama's visit she had to check in with Human Services. They were making sure she was doing everything she needed to do and for a while she was accountable for all of her actions. Mama gathered all the strength she had and took responsibility. She found a job and worked to get stable. The foster care system documented everything, including how we interacted with Mama during her visits to the orphanage. She did exactly what she needed to do to get us home. We never understood why Mama went back to Chicago to visit. We thought we were home free and away from the pain and anguish. Chicago had been a place that had created so many painful memories. 'Why had Mama expected a good time in a place where she had been beat down spiritually and physically?' Mama disapproved of our short hair and when we returned home, she told us so.

Mama blamed the orphanage staff for the separation of her children and later told us that they had originally prevented her

from seeing us. Supposedly she had gotten so upset that she threatened to "burn the orphanage down if they didn't let her see us". We weren't sure how true that was, Mama also told us that she had been kidnapped, drugged, and beaten in Chicago, but Nana told a different story, she said Mama had been with one of her old flames.

Chapter 9

Broken Souls

Shortly after we left the orphanage, and returned home, Los was released from prison. He had served a two-year prison sentence and immediately traveled to Detroit to see Mama and once again, he swept her off her feet. Our happy times didn't last, because they were reunited, which meant we were all reunited. Los and his family were suddenly thrown back into our lives and our strong opinions didn't matter.

Since it was summer time, Mama sent Rhaquel and me alone to Chicago as collateral while she finalized the swift departure. Mama met us in Chicago a few days later. She was just in time for the annual celebration.

It was the 4th of July, and a day after my sixteenth birthday. Los's family was all together at a park in Chicago to celebrating the annual picnic. These events, just like all the others started out fun, but family fights and arguments always erupted between the brothers. I remember not wanting to go, but we were never allowed a say in the matter. I couldn't remember the last time since we met Los that I'd had a great birthday. Something bad always seemed to happen in July. 'Maybe this time, things would be different,' I thought. Los yelled for me to fix him a plate of food. I despised him. 'Why couldn't my mother do it?' I was sick of him and his idea that I was his woman and I know it showed in my attitude.

He made me press and curl his hair before he'd go out on his midnight rendezvous. I'd practice burning his scalp from time to time to let him know I didn't care to do his hair. I even thought of getting some lighter fluid and setting him on fire, but I didn't want to go to jail for murder. I knew his intent. I felt his growing lust towards me, not just at the picnic, but he had become more ambitious. It made me scared and angry at the same time, and I felt the walls closing in on me.

Every time I caught him looking in my direction that day, I looked away. He watched every move my sister and I made. The tension between Los and I was thick that day. All my hatred had risen to the surface, but Los feared something that hadn't occurred to me, I was sixteen, I would get a boyfriend soon, and more than likely, have sex. It was inevitable. I handed him the plate with a force filled with hate and resentment. I couldn't pretend to love him as a father, or anything else. I didn't want him to be confused at all; I wanted him to know I didn't like anything about him. He snatched the plate, stood up in the presence of everyone, and slapped me so hard it felt like a fire-hot brick had hit me. My mother looked at me in silence and disbelief. Concerned that the commotion may break up the picnic, Nana yelled, "Los! Why did you hit that girl like that?" Mama jumped up and ran to a nearby bridge, where she sobbed without uttering a word. Los had clearly become the topic of whispers, and he didn't like it. He became furious and gathered his things and demanded that we get on the train and go home with him--- without Mama. Mama watched us leave; she had no say so, even if she knew in her heart what his plans were. She didn't say a word as we were whisked away by her angry boyfriend.

When we got to the apartment, we completed a few chores while Los sat on the couch and watched television. I asked him if we could go to the neighborhood party and surprisingly, he said "Yeah, you can go to the party," with a seductive grin on his face.

It wasn't the first time I'd felt like I wanted to kill Los. He had stolen my innocence. I had planned to save my virginity for my husband. I had it all planned out, I envisioned a fine, respectable man of my choice. I imagined myself walking down the aisle in a beautiful wedding gown. Never in a million years did I think my mother's boyfriend would take advantage of me and steal my innocence, but he had done that several months ago. My mind trailed back to that dreadful evening...

I had been out with my friend for most of the day. When I got home and our apartment was darker than usual that night, but Los wasn't alone, he had family over and they were drinking and smoking marijuana. Mama sat on the couch across the room in a daze. One of his brothers offered me some alcohol and I took it. I had never been drunk before, although I'd often wondered what it felt like because we were always exposed to alcohol, drugs, and addicts. I had promised myself that I would never be like the druggies we saw every day, although I often felt defeated, and was afraid that it was only a matter of time. Los watched and waited for the alcohol to work its way through my system. The more I drank, the braver I got. They didn't know that I had gone to a party earlier that night with my girlfriend and she had given me some valium! The valium mixed with the alcohol heightened my courage and I began to question my mother, "Why are we so poor? Why can't we participate in any school activities?" As I questioned Mama, tears rolled down my cheeks. Mama listened intently. I asked her a few more questions, and then I noticed Los gazing across the room at me with that anxious look on his face. While I was pouring my heart out to my mother he was conspiring against me and my innocence.

I knew what that look meant and was determined to stop him from touching me. He had been getting bolder every day and I knew it wouldn't be long before he tried to get me to go all the way. I planned to wear a girdle and body suit that night; those items would be my homemade chastity belt. I had been drinking and I'd taken the nerve pills, so eventually I couldn't fight my sleep, I dozed off. When I woke up my underwear was off and Los was stretched out in my bed pretending to be sleep. I was in pain and I knew what he had done to me. I didn't remember the details of what happened, but I know I had been raped. I was ashamed and felt unclean. I wanted to get a knife, but I was too afraid to fight him. I went to Mama's room and curled up next to her. I was too ashamed to wake her up to tell her what had happened. I had told Mama once in Los's presence that he had come into my room and put his tongue in my ear. I also told her that he had grabbed my breasts. She just sat there, not saying a word as Los laughed in my face and responded sarcastically, "What kind of a feel was it? Was it a feely feel or a squeeze feel?" He was simply telling me that my mother didn't care what was happening. I remember leaving the room feeling abandoned, and betrayed by my mother.

No one ever spoke of that night again, nor did they speak of the crime that Los committed. He got away with statutory rape, and no one said anything. We all just played it off as if it never happened. After he violated me, Los still expected to be respected, and even mocked me at times, insinuating that I liked it.

That was one of many times Los would to take advantage of me, but tonight I wasn't having it. Rhaquel and I had gone to the party and danced and talked to our friends for a few hours, and it made me feel as though my life was normal. We lived two blocks from where the party was, and we hoped Mama would be home by the time we got there, but we feared the worst. The walk home was the longest walk of terror I had ever taken. Los opened the door for us and closed it behind me. The apartment was very black when we entered, no TV on and no lights illuminated the place. My mother had gotten home while we were at the party and was now out cold in her bedroom.

I went to my room and began combing my hair, pretending to be busy. When he called for me I slowly walked into the living room, and immediately noticed that he had rearranged the couches and turned things around in a strange and different manner. He had a weird look on his face. I thought I'd gotten out of it and that I would somehow escape his wrath. I had started having thoughts of taking him out of his misery – and if I had just one ounce more of bravery, I would have. I sat down on the couch leaving a healthy distance between us as I nervously twisted my hair. My sister and brother stayed in their rooms. "Are we gonna rap, huh? Are you gonna let me pet the thang?" He said. I couldn't believe the words that escaped his mouth. I looked him in his eye and said, "We can rap like a father and daughter." He didn't like my answer and became furious all over again. He stood up and said, "Go to your room! You must think I'm one of those dudes in the streets." Just as I stood up, he slapped me so hard it felt as if I'd been hit across my face with metal. I screamed loudly, "Okay! Okay!" My body shook uncontrollably as I ran into my mother's room. Had she not heard me? I didn't know if she did or not, all I knew was that she never moved. If she was pretending to be in a dead sleep, it was working. His perversion had started long before that moment. I knew my mama was probably afraid for her own life, but at the expense of her daughters being abused? Even if Mama didn't hear me, she had seen what he'd been doing. Los pulled me out of the bedroom and continued to beat me. Mama didn't come to my rescue and he continued to throw blows to my face and head. In a split second, I chose to survive without Mama's help. After he slammed the handmade ashtray across my head, I pretended that I was knocked out cold. My sister came into the room screaming, and ran into my mother's room. She shook mama and even bit her, but Mama did not budge for us. As I lay there, pretending to be knocked out, I planned my escape – Los had gone too far. "Oh, you gonna' play dead? You lay there then." He said. He went and grabbed his pistol and pulled the safety off. As he prepared to aim the gum, I leaped up and ran for the door.

I remember jumping from the top of the stairs all the way to the bottom. I ran out of the apartment screaming and crying for help. I was afraid for my life. I ran to the gas station across the street, but the attendant turned me away, "No! Go away!" he said. I ran down the street, wandering like a wild woman in distress, my hair was all over my head and tears were running down my face. Finally, a neighborhood lady pulled up next to me and told me to get into her car. I tried to explain what happened, but I couldn't talk, I was on the edge of a nervous breakdown. She drove me to Cook County Hospital, where they examined me. They assumed I had been raped. The doctor checked me out and tried to give me a shot to calm me down but, I said, "No shot, no shot." I was hearing voices. My mind was playing tricks – I was certain I could hear Los in the next room ~~threatening me. The doctor gave me some pills because I~~ was terrified and inconsolable. I thought they were going to let Los kill me. Every time I heard footsteps outside the room, I thought it was him. I eventually began to calm down once the medication started to take effect.

Later that evening I was questioned by a female police officer who treated me as if this was my regular Friday night routine. She had no compassion for me and made me feel as though I'd done something to deserve that kind of treatment. I still didn't feel safe, not even in the presence of the police. I didn't feel safe anywhere or with anyone.

After I was released from the hospital, I stayed away from the apartment, except to take Mama money when she needed something. Whenever I saw my abuser, shame smothered me, and I was reminded of all the times I was devalued. To make matters worse, he smirked at me, as if he'd gotten by. Los sat in the living room and didn't say anything to me, I'm sure he was hoping I'd come back to the house. Sadly, Los' family was the only family I knew, and I had learned to be around them and to even love some of them. From time to time I still attended their parties, but in the back of my mind I couldn't face the fact that so many people had been silent about our abuse.

I wandered from house to house, trying to find safety and refuge. I didn't have much luck. I spent a night at my girlfriend's house, and her mother had to sleep with me just to keep her older sons away from me. I spent a few nights at my best friend's house, but the same sick behavior was occurring at her house. Her father touched me so quick I couldn't believe it. I figured I'd better get out of there fast, before my friend's mother found out that she lived with a rapist, too. Maybe she was ignoring it like Mama was. Perversion was everywhere I turned, and when I encountered it, I disappeared without any explanation.   Most of those places I landed were already chaotic and I didn't need more chaos in my life.

After living pretty much homeless for a few months, Nadine coerced me into moving in with her and she was able to get foster care benefits for me. The living situation was never healthy and I was still never really happy. After living with Nadine for about a year, she announced that she would be moving to Minnesota and that I was going with her. I saw Minnesota as being a new chapter in my life, I would soon be 18 and I was looking forward to being independent. It wasn't easy to live with Nadine. When we moved to Minnesota she had already been approved for a low income housing project in North Minneapolis.

Fortunately for me, Nadine didn't stay in Minnesota very long, for some reason she just didn't like it. She packed up her daughter and they up and moved back to Chicago without me. I made it clear that I didn't want to leave Minnesota, so Nadine left me in the apartment where I lived for a couple months until

I had to move. I continued to live with friends and attend secretarial school until I eventually got my own apartment. I floated through life until I was able to stand on my own feet and make a better life for myself. I lived for years in fear and insecurity.

When Mama moved to Minnesota I was excited that she was finally getting away from our abuser. To my dismay she had also planned for him to move along with her several months after she got settled in. So, there I was again, many years after my abuse, still subjected to seeing him. He attempted to apologize once, saying, "he was sorry for what he had done and he loved me so much, he went on to say that, he was a ghetto man with alcohol and drug problems." I didn't accept his apology. He and Mama always blamed the alcohol for his abuse and her neglect. I also couldn't forgive the adults who said they loved us and then watched us live in torment. That is until I had an encounter with God.

I was covered in guilty shame and felt inferior to every female I encountered, especially those who were protected by their fathers. Depression, promiscuity, suicidal thoughts, and anger became a way of life for me. In times of depression, I did exactly what Mama had done, and I became the very thing I hated. I drank; I smoked two packs of cigarettes a day, and even tried drugs on occasion. Every time I sobered up, the shame was still very much alive in me. I finally realized I was fighting my own past. I couldn't get away from it. Why am I breathing? How can I face tomorrow's agony alone? Those were questions that often flooded my mind.

I could have gotten over the abuse, I could have eventually gotten over Los, but the one thing that was hard for me to get over was Mama. Why hadn't she wanted to discuss my pain? I begged my mother to allow me to tell her my side of the story, but she couldn't take it all at once, she didn't want to hear it. Her denial angered me, but one day she finally said it, "I hate what I let Los do to my children." My moment of forgiveness for Mama came in this time of admittance. I strongly believe that she was finally admitting that she was partly responsible for the foul things that happened to us; the things she allowed. I wanted so many things from Mama. Things I shouldn't have had to ask for. I wanted her to be accountable; I wanted her loyalty, and protection. There had been times when the courts had gotten involved in our lives, but Mama always got to us first to coach us on what to say, "No, he never hit us, he didn't abuse our mother," we said. We covered for Los and Mama quite easily after being coached by them. We had to deny the truth even though we were afraid for our mother's life and our own. Mama frightened us with her motherly authority and told us to lie to the judge. She tricked us into believing the judge would put her in jail if we told the truth about what he had done to us. Each time, Mama's lover smirked in a cool, calm manner because he had escaped prison time like a vapor.

Los may have escaped prison, but he did not escape his suffering. It was clear that he hadn't been a happy man. He aged rather quickly, his health declined rapidly, and he spent much of his last days without strong support from family or friends.

Restoration comes to those who forgive, and it will free individuals to walk in their rightful authority. I am, and always have been royalty in the eyes of God. That's why the enemy worked so hard to destroy me. What the enemy meant for evil, God has turned it around for my good. My testimony will continue to be used as a tool to strengthen those who are hurting and overwhelmed by shame.

Chapter 10

Why Should I Be Ashamed?

What is shame? The dictionary describes it as a painful feeling arising from the consciousness of something dishonorable or improper. For many years I carried the burden of shame. I was in pain, I'd been dishonored, and what had happened to me was inexcusable. I was ashamed. How could I begin to deal with my internal hurt when my abuser seemed to escape all he had done?

No one came to my rescue. Child protection hadn't done much in my opinion. As a child, I couldn't tell anyone at school. I didn't want to have to deal with the shame or the stares when people found out about what was happening in my home. What had I done to deserve this life? I tried to erase every memory of what he had done to me, but I couldn't make it go away. I despised my abuser with the kind of hate that torments you day and night. Even though my innocence was stolen without my consent I tried to pretend it didn't happen. Many years later, I was still struggling with how I felt, but I know I was being forced to deal with my thoughts so that I could eventually overcome them.

One day God showed me a vision of an incident that occurred when I was a little child. I'd been sitting on a toilet, and Los, who was about thirty-six at the time, had bent down and peeped through the bathroom keyhole to watch me. I believe in my heart that this incident actually happened, and now God was using it to show me exactly how sick and pathetic Los really was. The spirit of the Lord said, "Look at him. Isn't that sad? A man doing such a thing is not well in his mind. That is a man without me." From that day forward I was freed from the hurt and the pain. That was the day of my recovery and forgiveness. I took the revelation God gave me and used it to forgive Los. Realizing that a man without God would do anything, I became empowered by the resurrection of Christ.

Like so many people with wounded spirits, my mother's troubled past and experiences caused her to live an abusive life full of desperation and unresolved issues. My mother lost herself early in her relationship with Los, and somewhere in her loss, her self-worth was destroyed and she settled for whatever came her way. But, her spirit had been severed many years early. That broken spirit overflowed into every relationship she encountered and it damaged her marriage, and ultimately affected her ability to parent. My mother saw the glass as half empty; she anticipated the worst in every situation. I don't recall her having faith in anyone or anything. I tried with all my strength not to become as broken as my mother, but the things I witnessed and experienced made that next to impossible. There were times when I was broken and battered. Sometimes I used the painful episodes of her life to make me strong, but there were times I failed miserably. Seeing abuse first hand allows you clarity on so many things and I was able to see warning signs in many situations, and in most cases I was able to escape them. For me the signs were very clear, if I dated someone who was jealous, controlling, or abusive, I distanced myself quickly. I've seen abuse first hand and from that, I learned some consequential life lessons. If I caught myself making some of the same mistakes my mother made, I quickly reflected within. Where is this coming from? Why am I allowing myself to be devalued? Who am I? You, my dearest friends, may have asked yourselves the same questions. Maybe you have been through the same sort of trauma. Maybe it wasn't sexual abuse, but it was something that could have taken you out, but you made it! Whatever it is or whatever it *was*, you can overcome it! Some of us have already overcome it. I have seen sexual abuse destroy dreams, futures, sexuality, mental health, physical appearance, families, and more. Sadly, in some instances there was no recovery.

By the grace of God, I have been blessed with amazing strength to have survived storm after storm, and come out with praise and power!! I have realized that I'm not alone, but I have lived through something that could have taken me out. I have reclaimed my strength and I've learned how to live in happiness and true joy. I've had moments of laughter, and I have learned that the power of forgiveness is paramount! Forgiveness has freed me to love whole-heartedly. I've experienced a man who loves me, and children who care so much about me that they were not ashamed of my life even when they read my story. This is my story. This is my truth. I lived through this terrible darkness, and through it all, many years later --- I realized that I was still lovable and I was still able to love my husband and my children. Today and every day, I choose to live free of torment or fear. I sleep well at night, and peace is mine. I have a reason to live, not just for my family, but that others may see my strength and hear my story. I need other survivors to know that even though they feel as if they can't make it through this darkness – they can, because I did.

We have the strength! We are truly equipped to live through all kinds of storms. We can live through high waters, low valleys, regardless of the struggle. We must climb the mountainside and go through rough terrain. Whatever it is, you can make it. You can be whatever we desire to be in this lifetime. So go on! Be strong! Pick your head up, and choose to have healthy relationships, you deserve it.

Every righteous prayer is received by God, and He never forgets. Keep on praying for strength and love for a generation experiencing much pain. Prayer makes a difference. Prayer reaches the unknown places, and it is accessible to everyone. Prayer releases an anointing that activates healing, deliverance, and peace to the believer.

My story didn't end in defeat. I chose to be happy, and now I have a life of my own. God gave me a man who loves me, five children, and grandchildren. My family sits down at the dinner table together. We watch movies, spend quality time together, and most importantly, we attend church together.

As a result of the life that my husband and I have built together, we have achieved happiness. Happiness that I knew was possible, even after abuse. In my home, we laugh and communicate with each other, we bring healing and understanding to each other's lives. Perfect we are not, but I can truly say that through it all, I am kind to my husband and my children and they have been taught to be kind to each other. I have learned to love in a world that was very cold to me as a child. My sons and daughters look up to me and respect me with a sincere love. Together, my husband and I have taught them to live in a healthy way. You too, can be happy and beat the statistics of recreating a cycle of abuse in your home. Just because you were a victim, doesn't mean you are destined to become a perpetrator. You have victory over your past!

I have shared my painful story in the presence of both men and women on many occasions. In so many cases, they expressed similar pasts, unresolved issues, and overbearing shame. One man even told me that he would never breathe a word about his abuse to family and that he would take it to his grave. My friend, silence is never the answer. Please know that when you keep silent, the chances of it happening again are multiplied in your silence. When we don't open up and face our truths, someone else will likely suffer. (Jeremiah 29:11) says, For I know the plans I have for you," declares the LORD, "plans to prosper you and not to harm you, plans to give you hope and a future. Guess what? *I WIN!*

Yours in Christ,

Sheila Perry-Calvert

A word to Survivors of Sexual Abuse

You have every right to expose foul play. It is NEVER too late. The longer we hold things like this inside our hearts and minds, the deeper the wound becomes. I'm not saying that everyone has to write a book. What I am saying is that there are people who can aid you in your healing. Pray to the Lord for deliverance from the shame and from your past. When we expose evil perpetrated against our youth, we remind boys and girls growing up in the same situations that they can be saved from this torment. Truth cancels out the fear and lies that are often told by the perpetrator and it puts the blame right where it belongs. We must not imprison ourselves for the sake of being quiet and covering up abuses, past or present.

It doesn't matter if a child is what the adult world terms as "fast." The adult is responsible for any inappropriate sexual acts or statutory rape. In my situation, my mother's boyfriend used fear tactics to keep us in bondage. He used threats to keep us silent, but he eventually had to face his own demons and live with himself, his lies, and all the unthinkable things he did to my family. It wasn't easy to forgive, but I made a personal choice to heal and to overcome. I now have the strength and the power to love life, choose my battles, and live life as abundantly as God's word says I can. I now allow God to use me to assist in the healing of others through my testimony. You have that same strength in you though God.

A word to the Strong and Brave

We've all been disappointed at one time or another. Some of us more than others, but recovery is solely predicated on how we move through the healing process. We can recover! Many people go through life never finding solutions for their pain. They try to cover up problems and memories by self-medicating with drugs, alcohol, sex, and whatever else they can find to numb the pain.

We must be honest, and acknowledge each painful experience we've been through. We must also learn to separate our emotions from our realities. We must realize that help is available if we ask for it. It doesn't matter how long ago you experienced hurt; it's okay to ask God for answers to personal and difficult experiences that you don't understand. There are professional people to help you process and gain clarity. You are never completely alone; therefore you should never have to hide under layers of self-pity, denial, or shameful choices.

Many of us have allowed our pain to catapult us into a place that was not ordained for us. That is why it is so important for us to find resolve and peace in our minds. My friends - please tell your loved ones the truth, even when it hurts. If they won't listen and take action, talk to the police or other professionals. Please continue to face your issues bravely with God's guidance and begin to seek and accept His truth for your life, for in Him are all of the answers.

A Word to All of You

We are responsible for those who don't know how to help themselves. Physical and emotional abuse can contribute to a lifetime of pain. The doctor can give you a prescription for the physical abuse, but the broken spirit and emotional pain has to be confronted psychologically. It also needs to be dealt with from a spiritual perspective. Sometimes you may have to remove yourself from unhealthy environments. Don't allow anyone to make you feel deserving of intentional pain inflicted upon you. Remember, if a person does not seek help for their outward expression of internal unresolved issues, you will most likely encounter another lashing out, often times worse than before. Eventually, your self-esteem will be slowly stripped away, leaving the abuser in control. You cannot change anyone but yourself. It is not your responsibility to change the negative behavior of another person, and you can't bribe someone into changing. Most importantly, you are not helping anyone by ignoring and hiding abuse.

You can't manage anyone's anger but your own, and even your own anger must submit to righteousness. You may be in denial, but you need to acknowledge the affect abuse has on your life or on your children's lives. Your children's innocence will be violated in the presence of an abuser. Never put an abuser before your children.

A Word to Parents

What is going on in your household? Parents, when you traumatize your children, do you really expect it not to affect them at all? Do you really expect excellent grades on their report cards?

Children are permanently affected by abuse, and in more situations than not, they will act out. Children will begin to emulate strange behavior. Girls often have relationship issues with boys, and later on in life with men, if they haven't been exposed to healthy relationships. Boys often become angry and violent, and though they are reluctant to admit the affect abuse has had on them, it causes the cycle of abuse to be repeated. Children often blame themselves. I have met men and women who suffered the effects of abuse, and never desired a healthy sexual relationship, not even in marriage.

Parents, we must be accountable for all the negativity we allowed to dwell in our children's youth. It's okay to tell them that it wasn't their fault, even if they are adults now, take the opportunity now!

Can you see Los through a child's eyes? Who was his role model? His mother told me that his father raped her when she was a teenager and she became pregnant. That was the root of his problem.

Children don't always know when adults are plotting and planning ugly things against them. They see adults as responsible, respectful role models who will do the right thing. I found out that if a person says anything often enough, it will become engrained in them and they will do just what they promise to do. Los did just what he said he was going to do and he ultimately committed premeditated crimes, and for many years there was no penalty.

As a child, I asked myself, 'When will it all end?' I didn't know. Should it ever be the responsibility of a child to stop this abusive behavior or be left trying to sort it all out in their mind?' Of course not. If Mama had experienced healthy love and the right man to love her and build her self-esteem, we could have had a much different life. I'm not saying that you can't live without a man, but if you're going to have one, make sure he genuinely cares about you are, and that he loves your children purely. We need to make sure that our children are not being forced to share their space with those who will hurt them or take advantage of them. It takes a village to raise a child and the village that raises your child should have their best interest at heart. Get to know individuals very well before bringing them into your homes and leaving your children to suffer from the emotions of a lonely, abusive and unhappy person.

Parents, pay attention! This is how the minds of perverted people work-- they plot against the innocent. They watch their bodies develop as one waits for fruit to blossom. They become fixated on their prey and carefully plan for the attack. Mothers and fathers, please pay close attention to the people sharing space with your children. Please be careful. Listen to conversations that are being spoken, and don't rule anyone out. Be aware when someone takes special interest in your children, it could be innocent or it could be detrimental.

A Word of Encouragement to the Abused

It was normal for me to hear of girls being raped, abused, and trampled over. I've seen beautiful women senselessly maimed, both physically and mentally. I've seen their attire change from St. John high fashion collections to trashy and unkempt clothes and hair. I've seen women use drugs to cover their shame and pain. If you know one of these women, or you've been this woman, share your story. Tell your testimony! Let survivors of sexual injustice know that they are not alone and that there is healing and deliverance for EVERYONE. Not every story has to end tragically; we can ensure that by speaking out and speaking up.

Encouragement for You, Sister Girl

We should never wish pain on anyone. Catch and deliver, no way! The commonly used saying, "misery loves company," is used far too often. If it causes you pain, why would you wish that on anyone? You know we all have different levels of faith and strength, and some people may never recover from the misery we "wish" upon them. We cannot allow women to be victimized in our communities. Let us care for one another. Even, if you've never experienced rape or molestation you still can strengthen those who have been victims.

I'm always blessed to know that there are children who lived and grew up in safe environments. It allows continuous healing and trust in a society where sexual abuse is so prevalent and often overlooked.

Encouragement for Abused Woman

Women who experience abuse often live in isolation. Abusers want these women to solely depend on them. When your spirit is crushed, it's almost impossible to be who you were meant to be. Victims of abuse often go to their graves never having shared their gifts or talents with the world. God created you for a purpose, not to be destroyed by the hands of a human. It's a tragedy when your life's purpose goes unfulfilled. There is greatness in all of us; it can be birthed out of us at any time. Every moment is a God given moment and is perfect for us to spread our beautiful wings. Be free today! In Jesus' name, be FREE! Escape isolation and meaningless relationships that destroy your greatness. You are worthy!

Encouragement for the abused child

Regardless of the things we were subjected to, I've never hated my mother and I will always love her. Most importantly, I am a witness that what God has planned for you, it shall come to pass. For every person who has had a tumultuous experience in their childhood, please know that your parents love you. For some reason they may have struggled with their own inner demons. Maybe it was domestic abuse, a history of sexual abuse, mental illness or hopelessness that caused them to be less than perfect parents. Know that if given better circumstances and a mind to seek God and to accept Him, things would have been different.

Encouragement for the Survivor

The odds may seem to be against you, but there is power in forgiveness. We are no longer at the mercy of our abuser when we forgive. We are no longer victims. We must own our strength, know our worth, and realize how valuable we really are. You can use your experiences and your "testimony" of healing to help others. Put on your armor and let's fight for each victim, let's help them to be survivors. You have ministry inside of you! Choose to be a better parent than your parent(s) or guardian(s) were.

Encouragement for the lonely-hearted

Single parents can successfully raise stable, healthy, and happy children. Children need love and peace. It took me almost thirty years to deal with my abandonment issues. When people struggle with abandonment issues, they look for someone to walk away or they are always waiting and planning for opportunities to leave. Security will come when you believing in your worth. You can overcome rejection and create an environment where there is peace and protection. Remember, God is faithful and He will never leave you.

A Word to Abusers & Perpetrators

Everyone has to decide to turn from their ugly ways. II Chronicles 7:14 says, "If my people, who are called by my name, will humble themselves, and pray and seek my face and turn from their wicked ways, then will I hear from heaven and will forgive their sins and will heal their land." There are many resources to help you manage your anger if you want change for your life. You must first admit that you have a problem and that it is your problem and yours alone. Change begins with the abuser admitting that he or she has a problem. The abuser will then need to seek help and focus on intentionally fighting the feeling of defeat, insecurities, and destructive behaviors. Most of all, Seek help!

When you began to have inappropriate thoughts about innocent little girls or boys, search your heart and seek help! There is help for you, but you must be willing to admit that you have a problem that is dangerous and unhealthy. Surrender yourself and call on the name of Jesus, I compel you to do so. He is faithful to hear you and to heal you! Anyone who calls on the name of the Lord shall be saved. There is nothing too hard for God, and YOU are not too hard for God to heal or fix. God cares for you. The God of peace and forgiveness will clear your mind and be your present help. Your true repentance will bring healing to a whole generation of victims.

Prayers

The effectual fervent prayer of a righteous man avails much.

A Guardian's Prayer

Let us pray and not faint! Father, release the guardian angels in the land. Let no weapon that is formed against us prosper. Our prayers will guide us into true revelation and divine victories.

A Guardians Prayer when unsure

Father God which art in heaven, I acknowledge your strength and power in my child's life. Help me to be a loving, nurturing, caring guardian and to be a protector over the children you put in my care. Give me wisdom and information to train up my child according to the principles in your word. Give me discernment and wisdom to acknowledge any problem my child may be confronted with. Father, direct me to an open door where I may find help and healing for any problems past or present in their life. Father, help me to be just when dealing with any person who has brought hurt, harm, or danger to my child and children everywhere. Father, help me when it is hard to face the disappointments of man. Give me an ear to listen to my children. Lord I don't want to be paranoid or suspicious; I want to know the truth at all times. Please give me a discerning spirit to know the truth. (1 Corinthians 12:10). Please bring

forth the truth today.

When a Child Exposes Abuse

"Father I believe this child is telling the truth; now, please help me to find healing and protection for this child. This child is hurting and ashamed, and Lord only you can renew their strength. Please help them to continue to cope with life while being strong and encouraged, with the assurance of not being alone, unsafe or abandoned. I cancel every assignment to destroy this child. Please release the angels of the Lord to encamp around them at all times. We put our trust in you and we will not be afraid."

A Prayer for those who suffer in silence

Father, I have kept this undisclosed secret all my life. I'm scared and too ashamed to tell anyone. I know I have a responsibility to reveal the person who abused me so they will not get away with this or bring hurt to another child. Lord, reveal the sins of my abuser and expose their wrong doings. Please grant me peace of mind. Please cancel all mental torment that has attached itself to me related to this undisclosed incident. Lord, heal me and help me to recover while I journey through life in spite of this unpleasant incident. Lord, show me the path to freedom. I have forgiven the person or persons for the assault against me, help me to move on in this present world with complete healing, and freedom from condemnation.

A Foster Child's Prayer

Father, I know you see me and have not abandoned me. Help me to have courage and faith to believe that I will find good placement, either permanently or temporarily. Please help me not to be disconnected from the new family you have arranged for me. I pray that they will accept me for who I am and not for what I've have been through. Please assist my guardians or my parents in finding emotional help for me. Strengthen them and encourage them not to give up on me because of any negative conduct or behavioral problems that I have. Deliver me from all forms of destructive behavior. Teach me Lord to respect authority and everyone who tries to help me reach and fulfil my destiny.

For the abused child

Father God I know you see all and know all. I know you have plans for me that are good and not evil. You have tried to wake up a world and cause them to change for righteousness sake. I know you wanted my guardians to protect me and when they didn't you gave me amazing strength to live, even through the pain. Jesus I know what happened to me was not my fault nor was it your divine will for my life. You made me beautiful and wonderful. The enemy has always been jealous of your creations. The evil one comes to steal our precious gift of innocence. He wants to destroy our faith in you before we even get rooted and grounded in your truth. Lord, equip me for the fight ahead and compel me to apply your principles and healing virtue to every painful aspect of my life. Purpose me to intentionally forgive everyone who hurt me and allowed me to suffer in this present world. I'm reminded that if I suffer with

Christ, I shall rein with him also. Lord please send protection to children everywhere and renew the strength of those who have been abused.

I love you Lord and I know this was not your intention. You have plans for every one of your children, plans that are good and not evil. Now I'm ready to face tomorrow with the strength of the Lord. I shall mount up with wings of an eagle. I shall run and not be afraid. I will press toward the mark of the high calling; I'm even more valuable now in my present state. For in my weakness God is yet strong. I hear the Lord himself calling me out. I win! I shall cause others to win also!

For Those Tempted to Abuse

Father, I need your help. I am tempted to offend someone sexually. I know you have a plan for me even though I feel hopelessly selfish and destructive. I know I'm in a dark place and only you can help me now. I admit I have a problem and I believe there is nothing too hard for you Lord. Remove this rage inside of me. It is not your will that I neither perish nor cause destruction to your precious children. Help me now Lord to not sin against any child!

Prayer for Deliverance

Father I am undone. I have caused great pain to a people, I know you are aware of all things and nothing is hidden from you. You are aware of all of my struggles. I need deliverance from unclean spirits, lust, deception, lies, incest, sexual disorders, control, jezebel spirit, prostitution, promiscuity, perversion, pedophilia, pornography, fool-voyeurism, exhibitionism, seduction, a filthy mind, etc. Whatever it is – Lord, bind the strong man. I do not want to continue in this pattern. I confess with my mouth and believe in my heart that Jesus is the son of God and He died for my sins. God forgive me of all my sins. I repent and denounce evil. Search me oh Lord, and create in me a clean heart, Give me understanding and power to keep your precepts. I will walk in deliverance this day forward. Thank You Jesus!

Acknowledgements

To my husband Anthony,

Thank you for being a great husband and friend. I love you. I know that I have been given this time in my life to be loved by a great man. You have always given me your heart and you have never judged my past. Thank you for your patience and support. Your approval means the world to me, and you have always made me believe that my ideas were great. To all of my children, I love you with all that I have. I am blessed to have you and my grandchildren in my life. Everyone of you are brilliant and you all make your mother proud. You have helped me every step of the way. Thank you for all of your hard work on my book. Your dedication to my story gave me hope and purpose. I thank you so much for your time and focus. You are simply lovable. The world is at your feet. Let the Lord lead you. The favor of God is upon your heads. Much Love Mom

Torie Chesney and Cindy, you both are visionaries! Thank you for making time for my manuscript. My gratitude is eternal. You're initial edits were very important in getting us here. You see, you hear, and then ideas come to life. I appreciate your ideas, they were very important to the final product. Now, look what God has done!

About the Author

Sheila Perry-Calvert is a native of Detroit Michigan. She is a graduate of Life Christian University where she earned her B.A. degree in Theology. She has worked in ministry for over 25 years. She has experienced working as pastor, evangelist, teacher and specializing in women ministry. *Sheila* works in ministry beside her husband, *Pastor Anthony Allen Calvert* in North Carolina. She is a wife, a mother and a grandmother. She is a profound orator of the word of God. She believes that prayer stills works! She conducts teaching seminars, revivals and *Sheila Perry- Calvert is* available for bookings. She lives a victorious life and is excited about her walk with the Lord.

Made in the USA
San Bernardino, CA
21 May 2014